HOW TO BECOME AN ACTOR

A Step-by-Step Guide to Starting Your Acting Career

By Theresa Layne

Copyright© 2015 Theresa Layne
Published by The Actors Layne Press
How to Become an Actor
A Step-by-Step Guide to Starting Your Acting Career
All Rights Reserved.
ISBN-13: 978-1519404183
ISBN-10: 1519404182

In accordance with the U.S. Copyright Act of 1976, the scanning, uploading, and electronic sharing of any part of this book without the permission of the author constitutes unlawful piracy and theft of the author's intellectual property. If you would like to use material from the book (other than for review purposed), prior written permission must be obtained by contacting the author.

Although the author has made every effort to ensure that the information in this book was correct at the time of publication, the author does not assume and hereby disclaims any liability to any party for any loss, damage, or disruption caused by errors or omissions, whether such errors or omissions result from negligence, accident, or any other cause.

PREFACE

This book is dedicated to you, the aspiring actor.

This is the book I wish I had when I started my acting career.

This is the book I want every aspiring actor
to read and put into action.

This book will help you avoid
wasting time and money and get you
working as an actor.

I have a passion for aspiring actors, spreading my wisdom, sharing my journey, and helping other people reach their goals. I just don't have the time to meet with every impassioned actor. I have spent countless hours sharing my knowledge with new actors. Now, I have finally written down everything I know about how to get acting jobs without wasting time and money.

You will find clear facts about the theater and film industry, as well as the opportunities and resources available. I do want to caution you before you embark on this journey. The facts are clear: a full-time career in acting is extremely difficult. Only a very small percentage of actors actually make a living from acting jobs alone. However, you absolutely can expect to make some extra cash and also have enough money to pay for your acting expenses if you take my advice. To do this, you must absolutely love it and not simply be looking for fame and fortune.

Theresa Layne

Since the film and theater industry outside of the big cities doesn't pay very well but demands professionalism, I have included all of my money savings tips for training recommendations, marketing tactics, and networking strategies. I began my journey with a very small budget, but with each paying acting job, I set aside money to reinvest into my career and generated a supplemental income from acting.

I am so excited to share with you all the tools I used to succeed. And now, it is your turn.

ABOUT THE AUTHOR

Imagine being in an acting class, performing a scene with a partner, and being more concerned about the success of your partner, coaching them, encouraging them, rooting for them... and when the teacher says, "WOW - that was some of your best work"... you smile from ear-to-ear with pride at the success of your scene partner. Well, that is me.

From an early age, I always wanted to be a teacher, not an actor. I know this may sound crazy, but the idea of living in New York, Los Angeles, or Chicago made me ill. You have to understand, I was brought up in Wind Lake, Wisconsin, population 1,000. The only reason I majored in Acting my freshman year of college is because I received an acting scholarship. Well, as a part of the deal, I was required to audition for *all* the plays. I actually got cast in the main stage productions, which as a freshman, is highly unusual. Then, I had to audition for a musical... I had never sang on stage or in public—*ever*—and they call me back for the lead in A *Chorus Line*... What? Thank God, I didn't get that part and got a smaller role, but I had to seriously consider becoming an actor. I was getting hooked.

The theater department at the University of Wisconsin - Stevens Point was an amazing place where I met so many wonderful teachers and students. There was only one problem: it was flippin' ridiculously cold there. One night after rehearsal, about 11:30 p.m., as I walked home, I nearly froze to death... and I am not being overdramatic. Okay, probably a bit dramatic, but seriously, it was -80 below wind chill and I thought, as God is my witness, I am transferring to a school in a warmer climate.

Shortly after nearly freezing to death, I did some research and found that San Diego had a lot to offer for me as an actor. The Old Globe, La Jolla Playhouse, San Diego Rep, Moonlight Stage Prod, and the Lawrence Welk Theater were some really great, strong theater companies. Not to mention Los Angeles is only a short drive away should I get adventurous enough to do the commute. Once I decided I wanted to live in San Diego, I auditioned for the School of Performing and Visual Arts at the United States International University. This was one of the only schools that had a Musical Theater program in the country. I received an amazing performance and academic scholarship and off I drove across the country by myself at age nineteen.

Incredibly, within three months, I had landed my first professional job in an Equity Theater at the Lawrence Welk Resort while I was attending college. It was gratifying, edifying, and oh, so encouraging having my first role outside of a university setting to be in an actual professional theater where I made *money* and it was a *musical*.

After graduating, I worked part time at Moonlight Stage Productions as the assistant to the wonderful and amazing artistic director, Kathy Brombacher. I taught theater to children at the California Center for the Arts in Escondido, performed in theater (some paying and some not), got an agent and worked a few training video jobs - just to bring in enough money to cover my expenses. Knowing I wanted to teach acting in a college setting, I set out to get a Master's Degree in Acting. I took the time to research graduate programs and thankfully found and got accepted at The University of Arizona. Their amazing two year Masters of Fine Arts (MFA) program offered a stipend and a teaching assistantship along with an incredible partnership with The Arizona Repertory Theater where I got to perform in many amazing productions.

HOW TO BECOME AN ACTOR

Being an authentic acting teacher and coach meant I would not only need a Master's Degree to teach at the college level, but I would also need current acting credits. I have taught for many years at College of the Canyons and MiraCosta College as a part-time faculty member. As I raise my children, I have switched from teaching in class to online which has allowed me the freedom and flexibility to continue to pursue acting jobs.

I have worked as an actor in just about every genre, style, and media from the musical *Dr. Seuss' How the Grinch Stole Christmas* at The Old Globe to the classics as Gertrude in *Hamlet* at New Village Arts to a dark and disturbing TV movie about a serial killer, national commercials, indie feature films, short films and internet comedy series. You may check out my credentials and demo reels at the following link:

http://resumes.actorsaccess.com/theresalayne.

Today, I continue to teach and work as an actor represented by the Shamon Freitas Agency. I am a former member of Actors Equity, have recently had both a commercial and theatrical agent representation in Los Angeles (just to see if I could do it - LOL), have Screen Actors Guild/American Federation of Television and Radio Artists (SAG/AFTRA) eligible status, and play drums and sing in a band… because I *love* it! And, if you love doing something, then don't deny yourself that joy. Figure out a way to make it happen. It takes hard work, but just because it is hard doesn't mean it is not worth doing.

Theresa Layne

TRAINING

Training is essential, but it doesn't have to be expensive.

The training I recommend will give you the foundation to handle any kind of acting job. Training needed:

Stage Acting
Camera Acting
Audition
Improvisation

Even if your focus is film acting, I still recommend that you take stage acting classes because it trains you to be able to handle filming the master and continuous shot. Watch this short audition reel for Project Greenlight by Emmy Award winning San Diego director, Michael Brueggemeyer. It is two minutes long and was filmed in one continuous shot with no cuts.

https://vimeo.com/105176169

For the best low-cost acting training, I suggest starting with community college theater acting classes. Look for the college drama or theater website and the list of instructors. Search their credentials and make an informed decision. If the college website does not list the instructors, go to the school's class schedule to find the instructor's name and Google them to find out as much as you can.

If you can't attend classes during the day, then research theater classes offered by local theater companies or acting schools. Regardless, you must research the instructor's credentials.

THEATER COMPANY ACTING CLASSES

By taking classes at a local theater, you instantly begin to have a relationship with the people who are associated with the theater. Contacts are *everything*.

ACTING FOR THE CAMERA CLASSES

When I was looking for film acting training, I asked seasoned, experienced, working actors who they would recommend. First, I suggest you sit in on a class and observe. Make sure it is the right environment and instructor that works for you.

While researching different film acting classes start by searching www.imdb.com to view the teacher's acting credits. If they don't have a substantial amount of solid credits then you may want to think twice about paying them for training. In addition to researching credits, you need to know if you will be filmed on camera and evaluated while watching yourself on screen. If the answer is no, then I don't recommend the class. Your best tool is to watch yourself and evaluate your work alongside the instructor. Eventually, you will transition into filming and evaluating yourself on your own prior to auditions.

FREE ON THE JOB FILM ACTING TRAINING

Extra work is going to be an amazing free training tool and sometimes you can make a little money doing it too. Extra work can be found through networking. Facebook and film groups often list casting needs through these online groups.

This is most certainly something you should do early on. Do note there is a huge difference between a young group of early twenty-somethings doing a short film and an established group doing a project. Do your homework and expect the unexpected. You will only do extra work for a short time unless you really enjoy it and then you can work non-stop. By doing extra work you will get a sense for what it is really like on set; something you can't get sitting in an acting class. In addition, once you have a solid foundation of training, I recommend you continue to be involved in doing student films, independent films and short films as a part of your continued training. I look at it as a free class. My perspective is these non-paying projects are a way to keep your acting skills fresh. Acting classes cost money and are important, but they will never be the same as being on set.

CREATING AN ACTING GROUP

Make this a quiet, secret group of actors you have met through jobs, classes, and networking. Choose a small group of eight to ten strong, trained, and committed actors who want to work together for educational purposes. I recommend meeting once a month for three hours.

You will need to have a place to meet, as well as a camera and TV to view back and evaluate each other's work (if the focus is film acting). Have each person supply short scripts found online that can be utilized for scenes. These can be for sitcoms, commercials, hosting copy, one hour dramas, soap operas, film scenes, etc. Basically, you are creating a way to continue training without having to pay for a teacher. Obviously, this is something you would do after you have completed a solid amount of training in both theater and film.

Create an agreement to be signed by each member stating everyone must be prepared, use/accept constructive criticism, and always be professional or they will kindly be asked to leave the group. This includes not dominating the conversation when giving feedback. If you pick the right people whom you know really well, none of these things should be an issue. Create a closed Facebook group for easy communication and privacy.

TELEPROMPTER TRAINING

There are wonderful apps available for phones, tablets and computers that can help you train yourself to use a teleprompter. You don't need to purchase an actual teleprompter machine to get used to the process of using one. Many *industrial video* or corporate training videos utilize a teleprompter for long scripts of technical material.

I trained myself by copying a description of a product I knew nothing about into the iPhone app ProPrompter, attaching my iPhone to a camera stand just below my camera with a clip mount I purchased on Amazon, and hit record. During playback, I evaluated whether I was able to sound spontaneous.

Practice until you are comfortable and confident. Once you are well trained, add teleprompter to your resume under *special skills*. I have found this skill to bring in a significant amount of extra cash.

I booked a corporate training video job and was given the script three days in advance. It was two pages of single spaced material with lots of technical terms. Challenging to say the least, but I worked diligently to have the material memorized and ready to go. The night before the shoot, a rewrite was sent with many changes and it was clear that I would not be able to film in one continuous shot. I thought they would use a teleprompter as I had used one in several previous shoots with this particular production company.

When I showed up, I realized the producer had scheduled four actors to shoot in four hours. Each of us had at least a page of technical dialogue all of which had been rewritten the night before. How they thought this was going to be possible is beyond my comprehension. Even if we had the script for two weeks, four hours is really pushing it. I asked the producer if there would be a teleprompter and she looked blankly at me as if to say, uh oh, I hadn't thought of that. I politely informed her that I would not be able to get through the material all in one take, but if she was comfortable with breaking it into sections and editing it together, we would be fine.

Honesty is always the best policy. It eases your anxiety and makes the expectations realistic for everyone. She really started to panic and made phone calls to try to get a teleprompter, but it was not going to happen. As a way to offer a solution, I suggested an app for her iPad, she purchased it, loaded all of our scripts into the program, and got through all four of us in four hours. This little app, ProPrompter, saved the day. There are many different teleprompter programs and apps available for a free trial and I suggest you experiment before purchasing.

NETWORKING

Once you are trained and ready to find work, it is time to start networking. You will want to have some business cards made with your picture/headshot and contact info. I recommend www.vistaprint.com or any other online company that provides inexpensive business cards. When starting out, you won't have much of a resume and won't need a headshot until you have built up your credits, so don't go out and spend a ton of money on a headshot just yet. I never try to hide the fact that I am new at something. I embrace it and so should you. I would get the minimum amount of business cards and have "Newbie" printed where you would normally put actor or actress or something else that is clever and honest like "Actor in Training." See the "Headshot" chapter for inexpensive tips and ideas on how to save money on your first headshot.

NETWORKING ONLINE

Start with a Google search for film, theater, and acting groups in your area. Search Facebook, as well. Set aside a significant amount of time to compile a target list of theaters and film production companies. Like acting group Facebook pages and/or networking groups for film and theater in your community.

48 Hour Film Project - www.48hourfilm.com

The 48 Hour Film Project is a once a year event that is an incredible way to gain experience and get a copy of yourself on video in a very short amount of time. (See Demo Reel Chapter.) Join the Facebook group and click on the link for the website and select your city. You can be put on an email notification for when the project will be taking place. Usually, it happens in the summer over a weekend.

The premise is to join a production company or group who will participate in the competition. Each group will write, shoot, and edit a short film in 48 hours. Once the films are completed, they are shown on the big screen and the best films are selected to be a part of the "best of" screening along with an awards ceremony complete with red carpet. Some cities have meet and greets or auditions prior to the event to help people network and connect. This has been an incredible training tool for me as an actress. Here is a link to a 48 Hour Film I was in that went to the Cannes Film Festival - Short Film Corner, *The Fatal Heir* (https://youtu.be/lBmu-jakSes).

NETWORKING IN THEATER

In order to become known in this tight-knit theater community, I recommend volunteering. You can offer to help in any theater department at any community college or for a local theater you wish to audition for in the future. Contact the head of the theater department of a community college or find the volunteer opportunities listed on community theater websites (See Finding Work). Introduce yourself and your interest in volunteering via email. Then, go to opening or closing night of a show. By doing this, you are almost guaranteed that the director, artistic director, or theater department head will be there. Yes, it is a bit like stalking, but less creepy. Introduce yourself and hand out your clever "newbie" card and express interest in their theater.

Many theaters will have special fundraising events, post actor talk back forums, opening night parties, etc. - that can bring you into contact with the people you want to meet. Directors mainly want to work with people they know, trust, and can count on, so get to know these folks and gain their trust through volunteering and then later shock them when you show up and give an incredible audition.

HOW TO GET THE MOST OUT OF A NETWORK EVENT

My number one recommendation for networking events is to bring a friend. It is better to have either an acting buddy or even someone not involved in the industry but willing to hang out with you to have by your side. This is the time you do not want to be shy. The best way to meet people is to introduce yourself and ask them what area of the industry they are involved. Be an excellent listener. Have your business cards with you and ask for other's cards if you feel like they are someone you would be interested in working with. Have an idea of how you want to introduce yourself. Don't try and hide the fact that you are new. Embrace it with confidence. After the event, create a database with all the new contacts you have made, log where you met them in the notes section, and what projects they are working on. Check out their websites, friend them on Facebook/Twitter, and send them a message letting them know it was nice meeting them.

Don't be embarrassed or self-conscious about being new to the industry. Be proud you are trying new things. Be honest and excited to learn and have new experiences. After all, life is too short to sit back and wait for something exciting to happen.

Make your own excitement and then you'll never wonder "if" you could have been an actor.

FINAL THOUGHTS ON NETWORKING

If you really want to make an impression, before auditioning for a Showcase type event, you need to send an email or Facebook message to each contact you wish to make. Introduce yourself and your interest in each of the theaters or production companies along with a link to your Actor's Access picture/resume and a comedic demo reel clip, if you have one.

The day after your audition, you need to send a thank you letter to all your target theaters, artistic directors, directors, and agents.

FINDING WORK

THEATER

I won't teach you how to audition, but I will teach you how to be smart, organized, and purposeful when choosing a place to audition. It can be very challenging to get cast simply because no one in the theater knows you. By networking and meeting people ahead of time and volunteering, you are more likely to get cast than if you go in cold. In general, people want to work with others they can trust and get along with. Most theater directors passionately love theater and love directing. They certainly will hire someone they know before someone they don't. So, if you want to work at a specific theater, you need to know everyone and everything about that particular place.

Create a list of theater companies that are currently producing. It is not enough to know the names of the theaters. You need to know how many seats there are, what kind of stage and whether they are Equity or not. Sometimes, Equity theaters offer non-union parts to local actors. Some of the theaters will have a couple of **"Equity contracts"** per season allowing them to hire one or two Union Actors. For detailed information on the Actor Unions see the chapter - Unions.

Be smart about who you are as a person. If you have a larger-than-life personality, then a bigger theater may suit you better. If you have a more subdued personality, you will be a better fit in a smaller theater. This certainly doesn't mean you can't do both, but you need to know who you are and nurture and train first in what comes naturally. You will have more success if you embrace who you are and train your strengths rather than focusing on your weaknesses. This advice comes to you from my own personal experience.

As a young actress I simply wasn't aware of who I was and how I came across as a person. It was discouraging when I would not get cast at the smaller more intimate theaters. If you simply look at me, physically I am tall and have a large frame. I take up a lot of space - just standing. Also, my physical life as an actor and as a person is overly expressive—you know the type—either you love them or they annoy the crap out of you. Well, that is me. Naturally, I fit in with the musical theater genre, the mystery café murder mystery dinner theater, the farce, etc. Isn't it just like us though to want to play the exact opposite of who we are? Training for opposite roles of who you are can and should be explored in acting classes, but honestly, you will be more successful accepting who you are and perfecting your strengths.

FILM

Getting experience as an actor on camera couldn't be easier. There is so much independent filming happening, not to mention all the opportunities available at the colleges. I already mentioned doing extra work, so now I will introduce to you the fantastic ways to get comfortable behind the camera.

College University Film Departments

Contact the film department head of any college and see if they have an actor file for the students. If so, you can send your picture and resume for consideration. The great thing about working with college students is the films get finished and the students are required to give you a copy of the project as a part of their grade. So, you are guaranteed to get yourself on film for use in creating an actor demo reel. Also, there is a deadline for the students, so you can be sure the project will get finished. I like working with the advanced film students as they tend to be more organized, serious, and mindful of my time.

48 Hour Film Project

As explained earlier in the networking chapter, this is a great way to get copy of yourself on film in a very short amount of time. Because the entire project happens over one weekend, you have a good chance of getting the needed footage for yourself. If you want to explore what it is like to be on set but are not ready to step in front of the camera, you can join a production company as a production assistant. Also, you may want to participate in other 48 Hour Film Projects in nearby cities.

Craigslist

I hate to say it, but there are sometimes acting jobs listed here. However, you should use caution, as there are so many creepy people out there. If it sounds too good to be true... it is. Don't ever audition in someone's home or apartment, especially by yourself. If they won't meet you in a public place then they just aren't professional and have different intentions. A true red flag is a weekly repeated post. In addition, some will post claiming to be a manager or agent, call you in for an interview, and then ask for money upfront. This is illegal. See Finding an Agent for more information.

Also, I can't state this enough, but always research the background of the people involved. – Do a Google search on their name and check for credits on www.imdb.com (mainly in independent film makers.) I would also include checking the sex offender database. Yes, I have learned many lessons and I want you to be cautious... always.

Always conduct a Google search of the name or names of the people involved in any project. I have had some weird encounters which I could have avoided had I just taken the time to do the research. Don't be too eager when it comes to Craigslist or Facebook auditions. Go with your instincts as well as research before you say yes to auditioning. Be smart, organized and purposeful with who you work with and why. You want experience, a copy of yourself on film, and to have fun.

168 Film Project-www.168film.com

A faith/Christian based film competition. Production teams have one week to produce a ten minute film. Sign up for the newsletter email and consider auditioning for upcoming production companies. This is their Facebook page link:

https://www.facebook.com/groups/168Film/

Four Points Film Project-www.fourpointsfilmproject.com

Four Points Film Challenge is an *all* online film competition. Get on their email list. Check out their site and see how you can network as an actor.

RESUME

Resumes can be done in many different ways and there will always be new and changing information as the industry evolves. The most important thing to remember is to be honest and choose a readable font like Arial 12. The best way to design your resume is to look at one and copy how it is formatted. You will want to have one that can easily be attached to an email as well as one for printing and cutting down to 8 x 10 size to be attached to the back of your headshot photo. An actual printed picture and resume is still being used as the industry standard for auditions, especially in theater.

Below you will see my film and theater resumes. Follow the format and pay attention to the details.

Start with your name and contact information at the top and when you get an agent you drop your email/phone and put the agent's contact info instead.

For whatever reason, commercial work is not included on a resume. The phrase "Commercials Available Upon Request" is the standard statement used. Interestingly enough, I have never been asked for my commercial resume and I have never made one. If you have not done any commercials, leave it off of your resume.

I would not advise pretending to know what you are doing. If you have a short resume or *nothing* on your resume, simply put *Newbie* or something more clever like "Wanted... Acting Credits Here" and include your training.

The section Training/Special Skills is for anything you do well in sports, hobbies, or an unusual talent that can spark a conversation to make you more interesting and memorable. I happen to sing and play the drums and can still do a backspin, which is kind of unusual, but more importantly, it's different and unforgettable.

FILM RESUME GUIDELINES

Determining what to call your film credit can be tricky when you are doing independent films, short films, and student films, especially if you are doing a series for a webisode. To the best of my knowledge, this is how you determine what your credit should be:

Film Roles are determined as follows:
Lead (Star): main character/appear in the majority of the film.
Principal: five plus lines regardless of story line significance.
Supporting: more than five lines, but important to story line.
Featured: under five lines.
Cameo: a star named actor appearing in a small part.
Extra or Background: no lines. Do not put extra work on resume unless that is all you have done. As soon as you have real credits, take the extra work off.

TV Roles are determined as follows:
Series Regular: appear on show under contract.
Recurring: appear on multiple episodes.
Co-Star: appear for one episode - character not central.
Guest-Star: appear for one episode as a central character.
Under 5: one time appearance with five or less lines.

Follow this format:

```
FILM
Name of Show         Credit  Director Name/Prod Company

TELEVISION
NEW MEDIA (internet)
(Follow same format as above)

THEATER
Play                 Role           Theater Name, Director

TRAINING/SPECIAL SKILLS
Class Name           Teachers Name, School Name
```

List sports you are proficient in, dialects you do well, dance styles you are good at, your vocal range if you sing well, and any additional interesting or unusual skills.

*As you can see for my films, I did not include the production company because they were independent films and relatively unknown.

HOW TO BECOME AN ACTOR

FILM RESUME

Theresa Layne
SAG/AFTRA Eligible
Height: 5'8"~Weight: 165
www.imdb.me/theresalayne
theresa.layne@me.com

SHAMON FREITAS TALENT
3916 Oregon St.
San Diego, CA 92104
(619) 325-1180

FILM

A Beautiful Day	Starring	Dir: Sid Franklin
In Velvet	Starring	Dir: Joseph Bolton
The Luck of the Draw	Starring	Dir: Ronn Kilby
The Heiress Lethal	Lead	Dir: Mike Brueggemeyer
Night Sights	Lead	Dir: Matthew Thompson
Casting Call	Lead	Dir: Giovanni Capitelio
Fall From Grace	Lead	Dir: Mike Brueggemeyer
The Love Trolley	Lead	Dir: Duane Trammel
What's Your Fantasy?	Supporting	Dir: Mike Brueggemeyer
Historians	Supporting	Dir: Mike Brueggemeyer
Letting Go	Supporting	Dir: George Ye
The Beach Bar	Supporting	Dir: Mark Maine

TELEVISION

Say Yes to Less - *pilot*	Guest Lead	OWN/Andrew Glassman, dir.
Lore: Deadly Obsessions	Supporting	DISCOVERY ID/Richard Swindell, dir
Peer Pressure	Supporting	UPN, Wheeler/Sussman, dir.

NEW MEDIA

Graigslist	Series Lead	Charles Maze, dir.
Fran and Jazzy: The Chronicles	Series Lead	Mike Brueggemeyer, dir.
Daily Delights	Series Lead	Jon Watts, dir.
Beauty Within	Guest Lead	Bryan Stratte, dir.

COMEDY

Dat Phan and Friends	Improv Troup	Comedy Palace
Improv for Indies	Improv Troup	Raleigh Studios

THEATRE (Partial List)

How the Grinch Stole Christmas	Auntie Who	The Old Globe, Jack O'Brien, dir.
City of Angels	Angel City Alto	Colony Theatre Co, Todd Neilson, dir.
Suddenly Last Summer	Sister Felicity	Colony Theatre Co, Nick DeGruccio, dir.
Talking With	Scraps	North Coast Rep, David Ellenstein, dir.
Moon Over Buffalo	Ros	Moonlight Stage Productions
The Goodbye Girl	Paula	Moonlight Stage Productions

COMMERCIAL/VOICE OVER/INDUSTRIALS - Extensive List Available Upon Request

TRAINING/SPECIAL SKILLS

Acting: Amy Lyndon, Billy Cowart, Andrew Barnicle, Mariko Ballentine
Improv: The Hinges: Adam Rudder
Formal: MFA Acting – U of AZ, BFA Musical Theater – USIU
Sports: Golfing, Bowling, Tennis, Ping Pong, Jogger/Marathoner, Yoga, Biking, Hiking, Snow Skiing, Ice Skating
Dialects: Native Wisconsin/Fargo, British, Cockney, Southern, Irish
Dance: Tap, Ballet, Waltz, Polka, Square Dance, Line Dance
Singing: Alto/Mezzo Soprano – Musical Theater, Opera, Folk, Country, Choral/Choir
Additional: Rock Drummer/Singer, Teleprompter, Juggling, Backspin, Moonwalk and Fan Language

THEATER RESUME GUIDELINES

Follow this Format:

Theatre			
Name of Show	Role	Theater	Director
Training			
Class Name		Teacher or School	
Skills			
List dialects, vocal range, movement skills, and instruments you play			

HOW TO BECOME AN ACTOR

THEATER RESUME

Theresa Layne
(888) 888-8888
theresa.layne@me.com
Height: 5'8" ~ Weight 165

Theatre

HOW THE GRINCH STOLE CHRISTMAS	Auntie Who	The Old Globe	Jack O'Brien
HAMLET	Gertrude	New Village Arts	Delicia Turner
NEST	Prissy	North Coast Rep	Jeffrey Ingman
TALKING WITH	Scraps	Actor's Alliance	David Ellenstein
THE GOODBYE GIRL	Paula	Moonlight Stage Prod.	Kathy Brombacher
1776	Abigail Adams	Moonlight Stage Prod.	Donald Brenner
JOSEPH…DREAMCOAT	Narrator	Moonlight Stage Prod.	Ray Limon
LITTLE SHOP OF HORRORS	Chiffon	Moonlight Stage Prod.	Ray Limon
MAME	Agnes Gooch	Moonlight Stage Prod.	Dan Yurguitis
LEND ME A TENOR	Maria	Moonlight Stage Prod.	Dan Yurguitis
REUNION	Donna	The Lyceum	Wayne Tibbits
SOUTH PACIFIC	Connie	Lawrence Welk	Mark Stevens
BOARDWALK MELODY HOUR	Ruby Divine	Mystery Cafe`	Tom Chiodo
SUDDENLY LAST SUMMER	Sister Felicity	Colony Theatre Co.	Nick DeGruccio
CITY OF ANGELS	Angel City Alto	Colony Theatre Co.	Todd Neilson
LAYING THE BOOGIE	Babs	Colony Theatre Co.	Barbara Passolt
LITTLE HOTEL ON SIDE	Pinglet	Arizona Rep	Dan Yurguitis
A TALE OF TWO CITIES	Pross	Arizona Rep	Harold Dixon
IMPORTANCE BEING EARNEST	Prism	Arizona Rep	Matthew Weiner
NINE	Madelena	Arizona Rep	Richard Hansen
SECRET GARDEN	Winthrop	Candlelight Pavilion	Tim Nelson
SOUND OF MUSIC	Nun	Civic Light Opera, SBC	Irv Kimber

Training

MFA - Acting	University of Arizona
BFA - Musical Theatre	USIU, School of Performing and Visual Arts
Acting and Improvisation	Andrew Barnicle, Harold Dixon, Christine Sevec, Doug Finlayson
Shakespeare, Voice/Movement	Diane Winslow, Susan Rush
Musical Theatre	Jack Tyget, Richard Hansen
Private Voice	Elliott Palay, Fran Bjorneby-Kramer
Film Acting	Billy Cowart – WCI Studios
Film Auditions	D. Candis Paule – Actors for Reel

Skills

Dialects:	British, Cockney, German, Irish, Mid-west, et.al. – can learn dialects quickly
Voice:	Mezzo Soprano – read music (opera, rock, musical theater)
Instruments:	Drums
Movement:	Basic ballroom, ballet, tap, modern (backspin and moonwalk)

HEADSHOTS

Theresa Layne

Having a great headshot is a very important part of your ability to promote yourself as well as a way to spend a lot of money. Because you earn so little starting out, I advise you not to go out and get expensive headshots taken. Even though a photographer claims to do headshots and has years of experience, it doesn't always mean you are going to get a good one. Therefore, it is imperative that you be educated and experienced before you pay someone to take your headshot.

ASK A FRIEND

If you know nothing about lighting and photography, then you should consider first finding a friend who knows how to take great photographs and have them do a photo shoot. You may or may not be successful, but you will learn a lot. One of the best headshots I got was taken outdoors by a friend who was an excellent amateur photographer. I landed my San Diego agent with the headshot below. I made sure to thank my friend by giving her a card and a small gift for helping out.

The two improvements I made on this headshot was I chose a better color for my clothing as well as a more business casual collar and made sure I faced the camera straight on rather than slightly tilting my head sideways. This advice was given to me from professional casting directors.

Theresa Layne

LIGHTING

Lighting is key for getting a terrific headshot. You want your eyes to reflect a pop of light or spark. If you are experimenting with an amateur photographer, you will want to educate yourself on a couple of techniques.

One way to achieve the best lighting is to take pictures outdoors with the sun behind the photographer, but not shining directly in your eyes so you are squinting. See if you can get another helper to hold a light reflector. A cheap way to make a light reflector is to use a silver sun shade that is used to protect a car's windshield from heat or a large white foam/poster board. By reflecting the light into the actor's face, you can get the pop of light in the eyes.

Good lighting can be achieved easily indoors if you have a large picture window where there is plenty of natural light.

MAKEUP AND HAIR

If you are female and don't know how to do your own makeup you *must* invest in educating yourself. I learned the hard way. After doing my own makeup, I was shocked at how awful I looked in a commercial. Immediately, I took action to educate myself on the dos and don'ts and I must say, I look better every day because of it.

One way to do this is to go to any makeup counter in a mall or beauty supply store like ULTA and learn from the professionals. Have them give you a make-over and teach you how to use the proper products. You will need makeup that doesn't reflect or shine. Matte is the key term. There are many makeup products that are termed camera ready.

Another option is to search YouTube for makeup how to videos. You will always want to bring a powder compact with you to eliminate shine on your photo shoot or on a film set.

WARDROBE

Color is very important. This advice is true for auditioning for camera work, as well. You need to know what colors complement your skin tone. I love this old book from the 80s called *Color Me Beautiful* by Carole Jackson It is a great way to understand what color palette looks best on you.

For men, I recommend *Color for Men* also by Carole Jackson. Choose solid colored tops that aren't really low cut since the photo will be fairly close up on your face. Keep jewelry to a minimum or not at all. Some agents do not like jewelry to be worn in a headshot and find it distracting.

The type of clothing you wear also conveys a message. Choose something you already own or buy something you would wear that follows the guidelines. Commercials typically call for a Business Casual wardrobe. This falls somewhere in between a full suit and a T-shirt.

ASK A COLLEGE PHOTOGRAPHY DEPARTMENT

Many community colleges have photography courses, contact the instructor by finding their email on the college's website. Introduce yourself and explain that you are an actor looking to experiment and get comfortable taking a headshot. See if they need a volunteer to practice doing a photo session. Also, ask if you could get a copy of the photo session shots for your own personal use.

DEPARTMENT STORE/MALL PHOTO STUDIOS

If you are not comfortable doing still photography shoots and don't have anyone who can take pictures of you, then these places can cost a lot less than the professional photographers, but you need to make sure you are getting the digital file on CD. Look for coupons and specials to help cut down on cost. You don't want to get anything printed from these places as it is way too expensive. I have had good and bad luck going this route, but I always learned something. Ask to be scheduled with the best, most experienced photographer or the manager and search for a discount coupon or promotion.

PROFESSIONAL PHOTOGRAPHER

There are so many great photographers who can light you well, but if you don't know what to do during the photo shoot then you still may not get a good headshot. That is why I recommend you try several other options and practice first before paying top dollar. The best way to find a photographer is to research and look at examples on their website. You can hire someone to do your hair and makeup, but be aware that you will still need to know how to recreate the look yourself when you go out on actual auditions. Imagine sending your headshot to a director and showing up at an audition looking completely different from your headshot because you don't know how to do your own hair and makeup.

WHAT TO DO DURING PHOTO SHOOT

Some people are naturally good at having their photo taken. I am not. Some photographers are great at getting you to relax and smile and some are not. It can be challenging to meet someone for the first time and feel comfortable sitting for photos. That is why I suggest you start with a friend. Just like being able to calm yourself before an audition, show, or film shoot, you need to be able to relax for a photo shoot.

A great guarantee to getting a natural smile is to have several phrases you can say to yourself that will naturally make you smile and set you at ease. You can use pictures of family members, puppy dogs, or anything that makes you smile and feel good. Use positive self-talk. Your inner monologue needs to be, "I love this…I am so grateful for having this opportunity… warm chocolate chip cookies… I love my dog… I love my spouse, partner, children, etc." If your thoughts are "I hope I get a good photo… I hate having my photo taken… I never take good pictures, etc." then you will not get a good shot. Also, if you have nothing going on in your head, your eyes and expression will look empty, too.

HEADSHOT PRINTING

I use so few printed headshots these days that I now will either have some printed up at FedEx/Kinkos or I will print them on my own color printer using photo paper. You still need to cut the photo down to 8 x 10 size and get your name printed on the bottom. I use Microsoft Word, insert my photo, and type my name at the bottom in a large font. Pay attention to the 8 x 10 size for formatting. Once you have a few credits for a resume, print it, cut it down to 8 x 10 size and staple it to the back of the photo so that one side is your picture and the other side is your resume. Invest in a paper cutter so you have clean cuts and straight lines. Always make it look professional.

If you want to buy headshots in bulk, you can use an online printing company. Reproductions is a great company I have used - www.reproductions-online.com. ISGO Photo is another one - www.isgophoto.com - both companies will do mail orders and have an online kiosk where you can choose where you want your name placed on the front of the photo as well as choose a border - just remember to use a clear clean font so your name is easily readable. These two companies have been around for years and do quality reproductions of your photos for just under $1 per 8 x 10 print. If you use FedEx/Kinkos, Costco, Walgreens, Wal-Mart, be prepared to spend $2-$3 per 8 x 10 print. Don't ever print your resume directly on the back of your headshot. Your resume will change frequently and you don't want to be stuck with an out-dated resume permanently printed on the back of your headshot. Stapling it to the back of the headshot is the acceptable manner.

BUSINESS CARDS AND MARKETING PHOTO

Once you have a decent headshot, it is time to start marketing yourself. Create a signature on your email that includes your picture. Get your business cards made with the same photo and create a Facebook actor page, as well as a YouTube channel using the same photo. Utilize a service such as www.vistaprint.com to create business cards for very little money.

SUMMARY

Your headshot needs to look like you—smiling—straight forward looking into the camera. You should have natural looking makeup and hair style and wear a shirt in a color that complements your skin. Avoid distracting jewelry and backgrounds. Most of all, add a pop of light reflecting out of the eyes.

ONLINE PRESENCE

A great way to legitimize yourself as an actor is to have an online presence. Lots of people will suggest you have a website, but not me. Only if you plan on moving to Los Angeles or another large city do I recommend spending the money on a website. My recommendation is to utilize YouTube, Facebook, and Actors Access (free membership level - headshot and resume only) to post your pictures and demo reels. If you already have a family/friends Facebook page, I would create another one just for acting and only post links to your YouTube demo reels/clips and any information relating to upcoming gigs or events you are attending - you can make a fan page or a regular page. Actors Access is a wonderful tool to utilize as an email link to your picture and resume without having to spend any money.

In your profile on Facebook and YouTube, be sure to include the link to your Actors Access page. In the future, you should consider creating a Vine Channel, as well, to post short clips and gain more followers.

You want to create a fan base of people who are interested in seeing you on camera or on stage. The more fans you have the more seats you fill in a theater or film. Often times a director of a low budget independent feature film will recognize the value of an actor who has a large fan base who would potentially support you in their film. It is also a great tool for negotiating higher pay in either film or theater.

Recap: Create YouTube channel for demo reels, create a Facebook page for acting only news and information, and create an Actors Access account to post a picture and resume. Consider Vine Channel after reading "Producing Copy."

IMDb - INTERNET MOVIE DATABASE
www.imdb.com

This is an important part of your online presence as it legitimizes you as an actor. When a student or independent film is accepted into a film festival, all the actors, writers, producers, directors, etc. can receive credit on the IMDb website. For a non-union actor, this is vital as it provides SAG/AFTRA casting directors a legitimate way to cast you in a SAG/AFTRA film or TV role when you are not yet a member. Many smaller cities may film union TV shows and movies and utilize local talent for smaller roles, if you get cast in a speaking role then you have the option of joining the SAG/AFTRA union. Once you have credits on IMDb, you will need to decide if you would like to pay for an annual membership called IMDbPro. I highly recommend that once you have a few credits and a demo reel that you become an IMDbPro member. Set up a profile with photos, demo reel, and resume. Members can search for pre-production projects specifically happening in your hometown by using the filter feature. Once you have a list of all local projects, send a notice to the producer or casting director. Introduce yourself and let them know you are a local hire and they will be able to access all your information through IMDb. Local hire is a term used when you work on a film in the same city that you live.

DEMO REEL

You will want to start collecting footage to create your acting demo reel. This will not cost you as much if you are willing to train yourself to edit your own material. I love my Mac computer and iMovie and have been able to teach myself how to edit video. This has saved me a ton of money. I like being in creative control and really enjoy editing. Having someone else edit for you can cost up to $50 an hour. For PC users, Windows Movie Maker will do everything you need, as well.

Once you have footage of yourself, you will want to start playing around with editing your scenes. I went to a demo reel night event in Los Angeles to view and discuss ten actor demo reels. A panel of professional managers, agents, and acting coaches all of whom had twenty plus years of experience in the film and TV industry evaluated and discussed each reel. The demo reel that gained the highest praise happened to have been edited by the actress herself. After speaking with her about her experience, she inspired me to edit my own demo reels.

Here are some guidelines:

*No intro montage with music

Creating an intro montage was popular in the past; however, industry people today feel it is a waste of time and they really want to see you right away.

*Keep it short

Your demo reel should be kept as short as possible. Two minutes is best, but I have seen five minute reels and I am left wondering if anyone ever watches the entire thing. Don't get caught up in yourself or the material. Take an outside look at the reel and don't try to make every scene have a beginning, middle, and end, rather make sure each different clip creates a beginning, middle, and end. Fading clips in and out can work wonders.

*Tell a story

Keeping the strongest and best quality clip first, see if there is a way to creatively tell a story through the different clips. This is a wonderful way to ensure the demo reel will be watched all the way through because it is interesting and each clip links together in some way to explore who you are as an actor. See if the different examples can be linked together with its own beginning, middle, and end.

*Scenes need to focus on you

Edit the footage in such a way that absolutely highlights you. Consider cutting other actors out of the scene, especially if their acting isn't very good. You can turn a terrible scene into something wonderful simply by editing out the other person's dialogue and only showing their face for a short moment before returning the focus back on to you. This can easily be done by separating the audio and linking it up after the cuts. It takes patience and perseverance. Sometimes the story can still be told without the other character's dialogue. You may be rewriting the story a bit, but that is just fine. This is another creative way to tell a story with all the different film clips you have. Consider the overall picture. This will take time and you will want to create it and then sleep on it and return to it with fresh eyes. Each time you work on it, you will get better and better.

*Each scene needs to show a different character or acting attitude

Don't use clips that have the same tone and acting style. Do your best to choose as much variation as possible.

TYPES OF DEMO REELS

Acting Demo Reel - 2-3 minutes including an example of dramatic and comedic moments.

Comedic Demo Reel - 1-2 minutes of you in comedic roles, choose the jokes, and edit to cut just after the punch line.

Dramatic Demo Reel - 1-2 minutes

Commercial Demo Reel - 1-2 minutes of you in commercials, "how-to"/corporate training videos.

INDIVIDUAL CHARACTER DEMO REELS

This can be an endless number of short 20-40 second clips. This helps get you cast into a specific role and is a great tool. Here are examples of some individual clips I use:

Executive
http://www.youtube.com/watch?v=pPz7cPl721I

Cop
http://www.youtube.com/watch?v=r3Tjw0LjDao

Mommy on the Edge
http://www.youtube.com/watch?v=6TSkwCEmpyU

Southern Accent
http://www.youtube.com/watch?v=vNMg5cvDuE4

Midwest Accent
http://www.youtube.com/watch?v=GrdyommABig

Theresa Layne

PRODUCING COPY

Training Yourself
Writing Material for Demo Reel

If you can make someone laugh, you can make them like you and remember you. So, I encourage you to create a comedic short for your own personal training and, if it turns out, use it as a demo reel product of yourself. Even if it doesn't work out to be a viable product, you will at least gain a tremendous amount of experience.

I recommend that you read the book *The Eight Characters of Comedy* by Scott Sedita. This book will help deepen your understanding of comedy, stock characters, and the structure of a joke. Be sure to evaluate yourself as to which stock character you are most like. This is an invaluable tool when auditioning for comedic roles, as well. After reading this book, I was inspired to create this short comedic parody. The clip was actually a part of an online contest and was recognized in the top three. The character was the Neurotic and the convention was the use of a series of Turnaround Jokes. The neurotic character is described in Scott Sedita's book as the character which is unstable and/or unbalanced. The turnaround joke is the use of changing the direction of a thought. For example: "I love that shirt…but not on you."

Watch this video: 48 Hour Energy Drink
http://youtu.be/FSH5HKqsTg4

WRITING COPY

I do not find creative writing to be very easy, but once I narrow down the parameters of a project, it somehow becomes more manageable. The wonderful thing about writing for yourself is you know who you are and what your acting strengths are. Focus on your assets and communicating who you are as an actor to help get you cast.

LIGHTING

Before you even begin writing, you need to decide the most efficient and easiest place to film. Start with lighting. Choose the best location based on where the most natural light comes into your home. Place the camera in front of the largest area of natural lighting such as in front of a large picture window. (Facing into your home with the window behind the camera) Film yourself, watch back, and evaluate. Experiment by turning on all the lights in your home, as well. Move around the room or the space until you find the best spot. Try not to have any clutter or distracting items behind you. This will also be the best location for you to film future video auditions.

BLOCKING

If you don't have someone to film for you, there are a couple of options for creating a short comedic clip on your own. By following the format I used in the 48 Hour Energy clip, you can create an interesting dynamic. The camera stays in place, but you will move from one area of the camera frame to another filming each joke separately and then editing them together. I went from close up, far away, left side, right side, and center. Another option is to create every clip in a completely different location.

SOUND

I don't recommend filming outside because of sound issues. Another tip regarding sound is when you are filming further away from the camera, you either need to speak louder or turn the clip's volume up during the editing process. Remember, you are capturing sound from your camera's microphone, so the further away you are, the quieter you will be.

WRITING

After studying the book *The Eight Characters of Comedy* by Scott Sedita, start with the stock character you would like to represent. Choose one you are most like, identify with, or have already played. Let's consider creating a very short comedy clip using the Dumb One stock character.

Line of Dialogue:
The Dumb One: I don't understand why I can't find a partner/husband/wife/date?
Watch here: http://youtu.be/dcEhS5IbSn8

Now, how is that going to be funny? Try adding a visual joke set up by having the character doing something unusual, strange, off putting, or disturbing like: while covered in cat hair with several cats on your lap, you deliver the line with complete and utter honesty or, if you don't have cats, use a dog dressed up in a tutu feverishly licking your face. If you don't have a live animal, how about using an assortment of unusual objects like a figurine collection surrounding you.

Switch characters with the same dialogue:
The Neurotic: I don't know why I can't find a partner/husband/wife/date?
Watch here: http://youtu.be/mvRf97oMTQM

Let's add this activity: The Neurotic violently shreds a carrot, slams it on a cutting board, and ferociously cuts it with a huge knife... pause... say dialogue while gesturing with the knife. Make sure the action happens before the dialogue as that can ruin the punch line.

Farts are also always funny and can be added for a punch line, too. We did an entire short film, *The Fatal Heir*, based on fart jokes and it made it all the way to Cannes Film Festival.

These kinds of clips are perfect for Vine video uploads because they are so short. You can add text to your video which directs people to your Facebook actor page, as well.

Once you have finished creating a short comedic video, let a trusted, talented friend who understands comedy watch it and give you feedback. They can help you tremendously. My first attempt at the 48 Hour Energy Drink short was not as funny as I had hoped. Then, a friend watched it and gave me some solid constructive criticism and suggestions. I re-shot it and it turned out so much better and I can use it in my comedy demo reel.

VIDEO AUDITION

Today, more and more actors are being asked to submit a video audition. I love this because it ultimately saves you time and money. You won't have to drive to an audition, spend money on gas and parking. What used to eat up three to four hours of my time now can be accomplished in one to two hours at home. Plus, you have control over what you choose to submit and it allows you to present your best take.

The challenges of creating your own video auditions are that you need to have a camera, a place to shoot where the lighting is good, and another person to read the other character's dialogue. The entire process will take about two hours if you are prepared, have the lines memorized, and you know how to quickly edit. Creating copy of yourself and editing small projects like described in the segment on Producing Copy is a big part of training for creating your video auditions.

The fastest and most efficient way to film an audition and submit it is with your cell phone. Download the YouTube application onto your phone, film your audition, upload it to your YouTube account, and send a link to the producer, casting director, or director. I would include a quick introduction of yourself (slate) before starting the scene.

"Hi my name is _____ and I am auditioning for the role of _____."

Try not to have too much time between the slate and the scene so you don't have to make any edits.

SCENE PARTNER TIPS

Ask a friend if they would be available for you to call on them for any last minute video auditions you might have in the future. Most people find it interesting and fun to help, but be kind, grateful, and respectful of your friend's time by making sure everything is set up and ready to go. Let them know it shouldn't take more than forty-five minutes to an hour at the most. Be sure the person you pick can read dialogue in a believable manner. They don't have to be an actor; they just can't be a distraction by delivering dialogue loudly and over exaggerated. It is very important you train your scene partner to speak very quietly as the microphone for the camera is right next to them. Otherwise, you will have to edit the volume making the process take twice as long as it should. Once you get to the point where you are making money doing these projects, give back to those who have volunteered to help you along the way. It doesn't have to be big; a thank you note and something like a Starbucks gift card can be a nice gesture.

AGENTS

You will most definitely will to have an agent. However, it is not the end of your career if you don't have one. You can find plenty of work on your own through the resources listed in this book. Click here to find SAG agencies in your area. Scroll to the bottom of the page to find "Search for an Agent."

Research each agency and find out how to submit for representation. You would submit a picture and resume along with a cover letter and a link to your demo reel. Each agency accepts different types of submissions - either online or through the mail. Check each website for their specific submission instructions.

An agent will never ask you for money up front, nor are they allowed to have "in house" photographers or acting classes that you *must* use. An agent will take 15-20% of what you get paid for non-union work and 10% of union work. You will not submit for representation until you have training, credits and a short demo reel. If after you have submitted to each agency monthly for six months and have not gotten a call for an interview, then you will need to participate in a showcase produced by an acting school or create your own showcase. (See Creating a Showcase)

COVER LETTER

What do you say in your cover letter? The best advice I can give is for you to be clear and concise. Do not make it too long or too short. Put your personality in your writing. Know who you are and what you are capable of doing for the agency.

Compliment them on a recent booking if there is something listed on the website that happened. Although I am providing you with a sample letter, obviously you should not use the exact same wording. This will give you an idea of length and what information you should include. The first paragraph should say something about the agency, who referred you (don't worry if you don't have a referral - but it does help) and that you are seeking representation. The second paragraph will either be about recent or upcoming projects you've done or about your training. The last paragraph is the closing statement about setting up a meeting. If you are writing an email submission, you can be less formal and not use the letter style format.

Keep in mind, however, that agents do not want you to call them. They will call you if you are right for their agency. Just because they don't contact you the first time you submit, doesn't mean you shouldn't submit again. Submitting each month shows persistence as long as you have something new to say about yourself and your career endeavor. Some ideas are to invite the agents to see you in a play, send a link to your new demo reel, or let them know about any new projects.

Theresa Layne

LETTER SAMPLE

May 10, 2015

The Agency
1111 Street
San Diego, CA 92104

Attn: (Agent name)

(Name of Agency) has such a wonderful reputation and I have heard great things from _____ (name of person who is represented by agency - your referral). She/he suggested I submit my picture and resume to you for representation. Links are provided below. (Or attached if you are asked to send a hard copy through the mail.)

I have been training at MiraCosta College for three years and have graduated from the Actors Academy summer intensive acting program. Additionally, I have taken D. Candis Paule's Actors For Reel audition class and worked on several student films, as well as participated in the 48 Hour Film Project. Our film won as the audience's choice.

I am ready to move from student actor to an agent-represented actor in San Diego. I would be thrilled to meet with you to discuss the possibility of working together.

I appreciate your time and I look forward to hearing from you very soon.

Sincerely,

Your Name
Your Address
Phone
Email
Actors Access Link
Demo Reel Link

DON'T GIVE UP - EVALUATE

It took me three years to get representation. I submitted letters, had referrals, and could not get an interview. I worked all over the place in theater, film, and commercials through personal contacts. My resume couldn't have been any stronger with a BFA in Musical Theater, MFA in Acting, professional theater credits, etc. However, doing a large showcase did not get me my agent. Instead of giving up, I re-evaluated.

My type, middle-aged mom, is not as bookable for an agency that already has a lot of people they represent in this category with my same look. So, how would I get their attention? I took a closer review of the material I had used for my All City Audition and realized it was dramatic and boring and I had only given a theatrical stage audition. Because it was on a big stage and I am trained to perform to the back of the house, I came across as a stage trained actor who would not be believable on camera.

After evaluating the situation, I decided to find a comedic monologue where I could use more subtle humor techniques. I read somewhere that in an interview you will be more memorable if you can make someone laugh, so I thought I would give it a shot. I applied some new comedic techniques I had learned from my film acting coach, Billy Cowart, and the *Eight Characters of Comedy* book by Scott Sedita and signed up for a smaller Actor Showcase in a more intimate setting.

The day after my audition, I received a call from an agency I had been submitting to for representation for three years. During the interview, I was asked to do the same monologue I did for the showcase within their tiny office. In addition, I brought my audition notebook and let them see how I track auditions and write down names and production companies, etc. The agent signed me on the spot and said they wished all of their actors would be as professional and organized.

PRODUCING A SHOWCASE

Sometimes you have to take matters into your own hands. If there are no showcases currently available for you to participate in front of agents, casting directors, or independent film directors, then it is time for you to create one.

Creating your own showcase can save you money compared to doing one put on by an acting school. Plus, you can keep the event small, short, and more enjoyable for everyone. One hour is the perfect length for a showcase with eight to ten actors. I have been to longer showcase events and feel that sometimes a really good actor may get overlooked. This showcase may naturally evolve out of your secret acting group.

Here are the steps to making a successful showcase:

First, you will need to find eight to ten actors interested in doing a showcase. Each actor must help out by paying a portion of the expenses divided between each participant. Next, search for a location. Start researching for an inexpensive place to hold your showcase. This can be anywhere there are chairs for viewing and a small performance area. If your event will be large, then you need to make sure actors will be seen from every seat if the location is not a theater. Have each member help to create a list of all the agents, directors, and casting directors you wish to invite.

Next, create and send out invitations four weeks prior to the event asking for an RSVP. One week from the date, send a reminder. Then, you need to choose scenes and scene partners. Scenes should be short and no longer than five minutes, be interesting and engaging, and each actor should be a perfect fit for the role. Each partnership must rehearse on their own, as well as create their own prop and set list needs.

Set up ongoing meetings with the entire group to discuss the order of the scenes and how props and set pieces can be used in as many different scenes as possible. Keep it simple, simple, simple. Give yourselves several months to prepare. Keep communication open and perform the scenes for each other for feedback. Make sure everyone is ready, memorized, and confident.

Have a dress rehearsal one week prior to the showcase. At this event, collect a number of headshots and resumes for each anticipated guest and put together packets.

The last step is to have some type of food and drink available like wine, cheese, crackers, grapes, cookies, soda, and ice. Keep it simple and classy. You may also need to provide a small table with a nice tablecloth. Before starting the scenes, welcome your guests as well as thanking them afterwards for attending.

Send follow up letters after the event thanking them for coming and including any upcoming jobs, projects or training you are currently involved.

UNIONS

The two unions for actors are the Screen Actors Guild/American Federation of Television and Radio Artists (SAG/AFTRA) for all media and the Actors' Equity Association (AEA) which is for all stage actors and stage managers. These unions are wonderful to join if you would like to become a professional actor. (See Acting Career Advice) There is a fee to join and annual dues involved in both organizations, but in exchange for the fees and dues, you are given fair wage minimums, become protected from fraud, mistreatment, and given the opportunity to have health coverage and a retirement plan. All the details regarding how to join are spelled out on the union websites.

www.sagaftra.org
www.actorsequity.org

SAG/AFTRA
Screen Actors Guild/American Federation of Television and Radio Artists

In the past, SAG and AFTRA were two different unions which merged together in March 2012. This new union is for all media work, film, TV, internet, etc. The only way to join the union is to do a union job. However, you are not allowed to audition for a union job until you are union.

So how do you become a member of SAG/AFTRA?

At some point in time, your agent or a casting director may get you an audition for a union job because the producer or director is unable to find a suitable union actor for the role. If you book a union job, you will need to make a decision as to whether you want to join. You can remain in an "eligible" status with SAG/AFTRA after doing one union job with speaking lines, but once you book your next union job, you must join the union.

Another way to join the union is to secure three background roles in productions under SAG/AFTRA contracts. This is often referred to as earning vouchers. Do not be in a hurry to join the union as once you do, you are no longer allowed to do any non-union media work. However, there is another option most people are not aware of, and that is becoming a "financial core" member of SAG/AFTRA.

SAG-Financial Core or Fi-Core is a legal option that allows you to do both union and non-union work. I encourage you to read through both sides of the issues of joining as a full member or as a Fi-Core member. Go to www.sagaftra.org and search "financial core" for more information. Read through the entire page. Next, visit www.ficore.com and read through that entire page.

Now, you have the full and true story and knowledge you need to move forward in making this very important decision. Talking to other actors about Fi-Core and the union is not recommended, as most people have not fully educated themselves on this subject.

So, while people are extremely passionate and outspoken regarding this subject, you need to think for yourself and make an educated decision based on facts.

PROS AND CONS OF FI-CORE STATUS

Pros:
- Can work both union and non-union
- Residuals
- Health insurance and retirement benefits
- Potential to make more money by working non-union jobs
- Keep acting skills fresh by doing non-paying indie films, short films, student films instead of paying for acting classes

Cons:
- No Voting rights or any form of politics within the union
- No SAG conservatory – may not attend free professional workshops available to SAG/AFTRA members
- No Film society
- No SAG Awards
- Can't run for a position within SAG
- Not able to use the iActor online database

SAG/AFTRA is a wonderful union and has so many resources for members and non-members. Be sure to check out this link (http://www.sagaftra.org/content/scams) to help you avoid being scammed out of your hard earned money.

ACTING CAREER ADVICE

If you want to pursue a career in acting, I recommend that you *not* get a college degree in acting unless you can graduate debt free. If you think later in life you would want to become a college professor in theater, then I would recommend you get a Master's Degree in Theater. Full-time teaching positions in theater and film at colleges are just as competitive as the acting industry itself. However, there are plenty of part-time adjunct teaching positions at many colleges which pay well, considering it is part-time work.

Another plus to having a Master's Degree is the ability to teach online courses. You could potentially set yourself up as an online teacher at several colleges and have a completely flexible job. This gives an actor the freedom to audition and work anywhere at any time. So, a Master's Degree in Acting, or any field for that matter, can be a wonderful asset to an actor.

Choose a college in the city in which you would like to live and work in as an actor. More and more production companies have been moving out of LA and going to other cities that offer tax incentives. Research areas that are currently bringing in cast and crews to smaller cities or stay where you are and make the most of what is offered.

The exciting trend in college theater and film departments is they are merging. As an actor, you should embrace both theater and film acting because you can make more money in less time doing local commercials and corporate training videos. Also, consider modeling as there are no lines to memorize and you can make some quick money to further your career. You don't have to look like a super model to book jobs. I am by no means model material, but I have been paid very well to do stock photography. As a model, in one day, I made the equivalent of playing the leading role in a semi-professional theater over a six week period.

Pursuing an acting career really means you need to be prepared to join both unions, have incredible patience, be willing to travel, go on tour, work on a cruise ship, live in a big city, and make peace with your day job.

THE CURSE OF THE LOCAL COMMERCIAL

Doing local commercials is so much fun, but let's face it, most of the acting in local commercials is pretty bad. As a matter of fact, a very talented and educated actor can be coached by the wrong person on set and give a terrible performance. Don't let this happen to you.

The process of doing commercials can make or break you as a local actor. If you don't know how to do your own hair and makeup, how to choose wardrobe, and how to rehearse, then you will more than likely only do one local commercial because no one will want to hire you again. I have been in over ten local commercials in the past five years. That is an astounding amount considering how many local actors there are in my city who are my same type. If you apply the strategies included in this guidebook, you too can enjoy the same success.

Here are examples from my experiences—good and bad—what I learned and how I avoided giving a bad performance.

ALWAYS MEMORIZE MATERIAL EVEN IF THE SCRIPT SAYS VO (VOICE OVER OFF CAMERA)

The commercial process for filming St. Paul's Pace went as follows:

My agent called to let me know I "direct-booked" the commercial. A direct booking is when you don't have to audition. It's every actor's eventual goal not to have to audition. By following the networking guide in this book, you too will make wonderful friendships, contacts, and business relationships with people in this industry. Getting directly booked is a great time saver, however, it usually means you have less time with the script. So much less time, that in the St Paul's Pace commercial, I actually was scheduled to film the very next day. I had to change my bright blue sparkly nail polish to a nice French manicure, pull wardrobe options from my closet, prepare a makeup kit, and reschedule previous appointments.

The script said VO which meant most of my dialogue was going to be voice over and off camera. I didn't bother to memorize the script, which was a rookie mistake on my part. Once on set, I quickly found out the commercial would be one continuous shot of me walking, maneuvering through a door around a camera and hitting several specific marks. (Uh-oh!)

After a moment of minor panic, I focused on what I needed to do to get the material memorized. Once in wardrobe, wired for sound, and given the blocking (where to start, move and end), I repeated the dialogue and blocking quietly out loud on my feet in the space where we were filming until we were ready to shoot. I made sure I wasn't disturbing the lighting, sound, or camera people. Most of the time, you will film scenes with cuts and edits, but every once in a while you will be asked to do an entire scene from start to finish fully memorized without much rehearsal. Without theater training, this would be incredibly difficult and stressful. I can't stress this enough:

do not memorize material sitting in a chair. You must move or stand using appropriate physical movements, as well, or you won't truly know your material.

ALWAYS RECORD, WATCH AND EVALUATE YOURSELF BEFORE A COMMERCIAL SHOOT.

Why should you record, watch and evaluate yourself before going on a commercial shoot? Because you need to feel and know what the parameters of emotional levels look like to avoid giving a bad performance.

First, record yourself the way you feel is the best. Watch it back and evaluate. Next, record and watch back an "Over the Top" or big and animated version where you give the worst acting you possibly can – like emphasizing different words for no reason at all. Finally, do an understated and almost expressionless version. If you have followed all the training advice given in this book, you will know what the best emotional level is and you can repeat it on set with confidence.

Once on set, know who the director and everyone else is on set and be aware of who is giving you acting advice. When on set, other people will sometimes give you direction. The following people have tried to give me direction on set: the commercial writer, the producer, the marketing director for the product, and even the makeup artist. The list goes on. If the director asks you to do it a different way, listen and evaluate what they are saying. They may not know actor language. Know that there is something missing in what you are doing and make small adjustments, but don't start punching certain words because the marketing director suggested you do so. This is an actor's worse nightmare.

This has happened to me on almost every local commercial set I have worked on. In one instance, a persistent "non-trained" person involved with the product literally pressured me to say the line punching a certain word to make it more obviously negative. I knew immediately that this would make the commercial come across as amateurish forcing me into overacting. (Commercials typically follow a problem and solution formula, but the problem should be presented in a light-hearted up beat way, not an over-expressive negative way) I already knew what the overacting would feel and look like because I had recorded myself prior to coming to the shoot.

Never be disrespectful on set to anyone who is passionate and cares about what they are doing. Graciously take their advice and retake the shot but do *not* do what they want; do it the way you know is appropriate. Nine times out of ten they will believe they helped coach you into a better performance.

You don't want to give the editor a bad take. I guarantee you that the same person who suggested the bad acting will choose that take when in the editing room. (Ugh!) So, the advice is to not give the editor a clean version of your bad acting, be respectful, know what good acting looks and feels like and have confidence in yourself.

HOW TO PREPARE FOR FILM JOBS AND AUDITIONS

WARDROBE

You will need to provide a selection of your own wardrobe to be used in local commercials and/or independent films. Most productions are on a low budget and simply won't have the money to cover wardrobe, so make sure you have a variety of solid-colored shirts and casual dress pants. Pick colors that flatter your complexion. Color is very important.

As mentioned in the headshot chapter, the old book from the 80s called *Color Me Beautiful* is a great way to understand what color palette looks best on you. For men, I again recommend *Color for Men* by the same author. The book is much cheaper than having your colors done by a professional colorist. Stay within your budget.

After reading the book, I went to the craft store and purchased a variety of colored paper. I took each paper and put it up to my face, just under my chin while wearing no makeup. If a color made my complexion look amazing, it went in the *yes* pile. If I wasn't sure about the shade, it went in the *no* pile.

Lighting is important so do this in front of as much natural light as possible. I took a large mirror outside. If you still have trouble, invite a friend over to help you. If you waiver, it goes in the *no* pile. You only want to have colors that look amazing on you and flatter your overall appearance. Finally, cut out smaller squares of your best colors to take shopping with you.

In addition to color, the cut of clothing can also make you look amazing or simply okay. Another great book I recommend is *Dress Your Best* by Clinton Kelly and Stacey London. You always want to look your best, so take the time to educate yourself and find out what you need to purchase when shopping for wardrobe. This will boost your overall confidence.

MAKEUP

If you are a female, you need to educate yourself on what camera-ready makeup looks like. You can hire a professional to teach you and educate you on the best products and colors, read up on it on the internet, and/or go to a makeup counter at the mall or beauty supply store like ULTA. Many times, I have had to do my own makeup and hair for commercials and short indie films and you will need to be prepared for this, as well. You should always carry a powder compact to eliminate shine to all auditions and gigs. Recently, I purchased a small compact curling iron because even though the job had a hair and makeup artist, they did not do my hair. I have very thin fine hair which loses its shape quickly. I didn't have any way to make my hair look nice and now I have a local commercial circulating with a really disgusting hairdo. Learn from my mistakes. Even if a makeup artist is present, bring a small kit of makeup and hair products.

PREPARATION

Snacks, Water, Folding Chair, Cash/Quarters, Headshots and Resumes - These items should be readily available for auditions or film shoots. Even if they tell you they will provide food and beverages on set, bring your own, especially if you have specific dietary needs or food allergies. The last thing you want is to be thirsty and hungry all day and night. The quarters are for parking meters.

CONFIDENCE

In your audition, it is your job to solve their problem, which is to find the best person for the role. Your job is to convince them you can handle the role, are reliable and will show up on time, are organized, and a team player. All of these qualities will come from your ability to be confident. Confidence comes from training, preparation, and doing everything you can to remain calm, cool, and collected. Deep breathing, encouraging words, and perspective are key to controlling anxiety, excitement and adrenalin.

When it comes to reality TV shows, we either love them or hate them. An excellent book, Me On TV: *The First Ever Kick-Ass Guide To Get You On Any Reality Show,* by Sarah Monson, is a great resource not only if you are considering doing reality TV, but also for techniques booking any open call audition. An open call audition means anyone can try out. Reality TV shows are non-union and cater to the untrained actor. However, for the trained actor, opportunities and connections can be made. Doing reality TV is a personal choice only you can make. The shows require improvisational skills and do have rough scripts with stereotype characters all of which is explained in detail in the recommended book.

NEGOTIATING PAY

Camera

When searching for camera work without an agent, you will know ahead of time whether the job will pay or not. Most jobs posted on Facebook are going to be independent no budget projects. Taking a job for no pay is completely up to you, but you need to be discerning. Ask yourself these questions:

Do I have any gut feelings about the project or people that are negative?
Are the people involved organized and experienced?
Will I get a copy for my demo reel?
Do I need this character type for my reel or do I already have something similar?
Does the project fit in my schedule?

You will meet people while networking who may offer you a job and ask you what you want to be paid. I have coached so many people and give this same advice. Choose a number that would make you feel like it was a positive experience and worth your time. That is different for everyone. If it is a non-union commercial with dialogue and the client will be able to use it forever, and they only offer you $150 for a day, I would not feel like it was a positive experience. However, I have done a lot of commercials, I have a website with demo reels and a Master's Degree in Acting. I have negotiation power. If the pay seems too low and you have a gut feeling that you are being taken advantage of, then speak up. Use your negotiating skills. I told a client/friend that I could do a commercial for $500 minimum. He balked at the number and said his producer wouldn't pay that much. I suggested he forward my website to the producer, have him look at my demo reels, and stress the fact that I am a professional and have a Master's Degree in Acting. The producer agreed to the $500.

Theater

Most of the time for non-union theater work, the pay is determined prior to auditioning. If you book a leading role and you know the theater is large and successful and you have a big Facebook following of friends and family that will come and see you on stage, you have negotiating power. Once you are offered a role, the director wants you, so ask, the only thing they can do is say no and then you can decide. But, if you never ask and you find out later that someone else negotiated more pay for a smaller role, you really can't complain.

ACTOR'S 10 STEPS TO SUCCESS

Today's Date:_____

One year from this date, look back on this action sheet and see the progress you have made.

STEP 1 - TRAINING

Scene Study

_____
_____
_____

Improvisation

_____
_____
_____

Film Acting and Audition

_____
_____
_____

Theater Audition

_____
_____

Research the recommended classes, choose those that are convenient for you to get to, are within your budget, and sit in on several sessions over the next month. Give yourself a month to find the right teacher. Then, sign up. Over the next year, you will want to accomplish the basic acting skills through scene study and improvisation. These both should be a part of your initial training.

After you have the basic skills, take theater audition classes as this is very different than acting in scenes if you plan on auditioning for any plays. Having a couple of plays on your resume is an excellent way to legitimize yourself as an actor. It builds confidence in film producers and commercial casting directors.

During the time you are doing plays, go ahead and sign up for film acting classes. After you have built a solid understanding of the way film acting works, take an audition course, as well. Now, you are ready to get some credits by using the resources I have provided.

_____ Research teleprompter programs and practice using a teleprompter on your computer, phone or tablet.

STEP 2 - HEADSHOT
Decide on Budget: _____

Contact possible amateur photographers for practice photo shoot:

_____
_____
_____

Schedule a photo shoot through a retail photo chain like JCPenney

_____

_____

_____

Possible Professional Photographers - Research

_____

_____

_____

*Review Headshot Chapter and prepare. First, practice with amateur photographer, if you get a great shot wonderful, start using it for your business cards, Facebook profile, email signature and 8 x 10 headshot. Otherwise, move on to the next step. Eventually, you will want to get a professional headshot.

STEP 3 - RESUME

Create your resume and update it regularly as you book new jobs.

As soon as you start training, you have something to put on your resume. Don't disregard any performance no matter how small or insignificant you may think it is. In the beginning, you include anything and everything, and then, once you get better credits, you remove the ones that were either old or very insignificant.

*For example: If at the end of an acting course you performed scenes in front of an audience, you can give it a name and put it on your resume. Create a performance at your home for family and friends, give it a title and put it on your resume. If you are a student and did an improvisation

performance in school during lunch, you should count it as a credit. Give it a name if it didn't have one - like your High School name and Improv Show, etc. Be creatively honest.

STEP 4 - NETWORKING
Check off the following once completed:

____ Business Cards
____ 8 x 10 Headshot Prints
____ Email Signature with Picture
____ Facebook Fan Page for Acting Only - Use Headshot

Join, like, and check out or start a local Facebook group to collaborate with other actors in your hometown. Look for Facebook pages of local casting directors.

Write in groups you have joined
_____
_____
_____
_____
_____

Attend group meetings/events:
BRING BUSINESS CARDS

_____ Date: _____
_____ Date: _____
_____ Date: _____

Contact the following theaters to begin volunteering:

_____

_____

_____

____ Create Actor Notebook

Create an audition/events notebook where you can keep headshots and resumes and a log of who you meet and where as well as auditions. After a networking event, place all the business cards you collected or names you wrote down in the notebook. If you use your phone, have a specific place where you keep everything organized electronically.

STEP 5 - FINDING WORK

Search for Theater Jobs posted online, write websites here:

_____

_____

_____

Search for Film Jobs:
____ Submit picture/resume to college film department
____ Craigslist (be cautious)
____ Check Facebook Groups for job postings

STEP 6 - ONLINE PRESENCE

____ Join IMDbPro.com and create an actor profile, upload demo reel and pictures

HOW TO BECOME AN ACTOR

____ Join and create actor profile on Actors Access (FREE) version actorsaccess.com
    ____ Set up actor profile on Actors Access
    ____ Create link on Actors Access to your actor profile
    ____ Add Actors Access link to your Actor Facebook page

>(Click MY TOOLS - select Custom Link)
>Here is an example of mine:
>resumes.actorsaccess.com/theresalayne

*Note: this is a long URL address, instead of pasting it in an email to perspective casting directors or agents, it would be better to use ADD LINK option to the text <u>Click Here</u> to view my picture/resume. Highlight click here and right click for the drop down menu to select ADD LINK - then put your LONG address in the box - just makes it cleaner and more professional.

STEP 7 - DEMO REEL

    ____ Research editing software for your computer
    ____ Learn how to edit and use software
    ____ Film yourself and practice editing
    ____ Make sure you get copy of your film acting projects
    ____ Create a YouTube channel
    ____ Create Short Actor Clip of first copy and post to YouTube
    ____ Create Clips of specific types of characters - use labels
    ____ Create Demo Reel
    ____ Create Comedic Demo Reel
    ____ Create Dramatic Demo Reel
    ____ Start a Vine and Instagram Channel

STEP 8 - AGENT

Search for SAG/AFTRA franchised agents in your area. List them here:

_____

_____

_____

_____

_____

_____

Set a date when you will contact agents for representation:

(Usually one year after consistent training and a few months before a showcase or the All City Audition)

_____ Date

STEP 9 - SHOWCASE PREPARATION

Date of Event: _____

_____ Send Agent Submissions monthly for at least three months prior to event

_____ Send Letter/email one week before event. Let the agency know you are seeking representation and will be participating in the event.

_____ Follow Up Letter after event. Thank them for coming and express an interest in meeting with them to discuss working together.

STEP 10 - PRODUCING A SHOWCASE

Date of Event: _____
Date of Dress Rehearsal: _____

____ Find 8-10 Actors to Participate
____ Find Location for Event
____ Create Invitation
____ Send Invitation to Agents, Directors, Casting Directors
____ Rehearse Scenes
____ Props and Set List
____ Wine, Cheese, Soda, Ice, Cookies, Grapes
____ Table & Table Cloth
____ Create Headshot Packages for each guest
____ Reminder emails
____ Follow Up Letters

DON'T GIVE UP - EVALUATE - TRAIN - WORK HARD

THANK YOU

Thank you so much for allowing me to be a part of your success. I do ask that you not share this book directly with others and encourage them to support my hard work, time, and effort by purchasing their own. This book is for you, for your journey, and I am so proud and honored to have been a part of the process. I love to hear success and challenges and would love to respond to any questions or concerns you may have. Go to my website blog and post a question any time. I will do my best to answer quickly and intelligently. Again, thank you for your support.

Make sure you check out my resources page for my top recommended books and websites:

http://www.theresalayne.com/resources

Made in the USA
Monee, IL
25 November 2021

83032150R00046